I0007813

Sommario

Intro

Every application, whether it is a Web application or not, is built on multiple levels to help developers organize the development of each feature. In the nineties the *two-tier architecture* was very widespread. Two-tier architecture is a simple client-server architecture in which a client connects to a server to use a service. In this way the server allows to share resources between various clients using a protocol that can be clear or encrypted.

In the new millennium, three-tier software architectures, also known as three-tiers, have become increasingly widespread, showing similarities to the MVC pattern (Model - View - Controller). This type of architecture is composed of: a presentation level (the highest) that presents information to the user; the application level also called business logic that performs the calculations and coordinates the entire application, performing logical evaluations; and the data level (the lowest) which represents the place where the information is stored and from which it is retrieved and therefore traceable back to the database used.

In this book we will start from the definition of Database, how many and what types of databases exist and in particular we will deepen one of the most used: MySQL.

The book starts with the installation and configuration to get to advanced queries, passing through the administration console. We will examine the advantages of MySQL and when it is convenient to use it, the SQL syntax and how to create databases and tables with data relationships.

A book for beginners

As highlighted in the introduction, this book is aimed primarily at developers who want to enrich their knowledge on MySQL or who simply want to use this kind database.

This book is also dedicated to those who want to create a site via Joomla, Wordpress or Drupal as they use MySQL as well as the LAMP platform (Linux, Apache, MySQL, Perl / Python / PHP) to build a Web App.

Show me the code

In this book we will use different fonts and styles to indicate different types of information.

Command line input and output for MySQL appear as follows:

```
SELECT * FROM user WHERE id = 12;
```

The Terminal input appears as follows:

cd /tmp/

New terms, important words, folders or directories and interface elements are shown in *italics*.

Requirements

There are no special requirements for using MySQL on your PC. We will use version 8.0 which may not be available for some operating systems. Please check at the following link (https://www.mysql.com/it/support/supportedplatforms/database.html) if your operating system is supported, if it's not, you can still use version 5.7.

In case you have to use version 5.7, you will not have some new features such as roles, hidden indexes, character sets and default collation but these are advanced features that we will not cover in this book.

Basics

What's a Database?

A database is a set of homogeneous and structured data, stored in an electronic computer. Therefore, it is an electronic "file" with many more functions and better performances than a traditional one.

Through a well designed database it is possible to access, manipulate, update and delete data in a very simple way and in short time.

Just think of the applications that surround us, our e-mail client, social networks, apps on our smartphone: all of them use a database to store data.

In this aspect, the Web has started the development of new generations of databases that make the use of the same resources by several users really efficient.

A database is also capable of performing complex operations, as we'll see in later chapters, for example aggregations and / or ordering of returned data, even involving multiple tables.

You can also update records in a single block, even millions of records in a single transaction, create relationships between the tables to retrieve a customer's orders or calculate the average amount of each purchase.

In my computer career, I even found entire programs written in databases. This highlights the importance of this tool.

Database types

Now that we know what a database is, let's see how many different types exist and what they are.

In essence, all the categories lead back to two macro-categories: relational databases and non-relational databases.

SQL

Relational databases, also called SQL databases, are the best known and widespread even in large enterprise contexts and, as evidenced by the etymology of the word, refer to the relationships between the data.

This type of model organization is suitable for organizing data in tables that are usually composed of rows (also called records or tuples) and columns and with a single primary key for each row.

The tables, as can be inferred, represent the entities of the application (for example Customer and Order) while each row represents a different instance of the entity (for example Phil Rossi is an instance of Customer).

Instances can be linked together through unique keys which therefore represent an identity constraint.

Some examples of relational databases are: MySQL, Oracle, DB2, Microsoft SQL Server and MariaDB.

Below is a table showing pros and cons of relational databases:

Pros	Cons
Structured data	Semi-structured data are hard to manage
Native management of data integrity	Data normalization
Constraints due to relationships	Scalability

NoSQL

Non-relational databases, also known as NoSQL databases, have had widespread use and development thanks to Web 2.0 and are mainly used for real-time applications, such as financial apps like stock market performance or big data applications.

These databases support SQL syntax but work best where relational databases lacks, for example, with semi-structured data such as XML or when performance needs to be really high in order to manage a large number of users.

The NoSQL databases consist of 4 distinct categories:

- *Key-value stores* where each element of the database is historicized by means of a key or an attribute together with its own value;
- *Wide-column stores* historicizes the set of data as columns and not as rows, therefore particularly suitable for large data sets;
- *Document* maps each key with a data structure called document which, in turn, can contain a document or several key-value type structures, key-array of values;
- *Graphs* usually used for information on networks.

This type of database is easily scalable, economical and easy to maintain but places a limit on both data consistency and referential integrity. This limit allows faster queries and insertions but results in a propagation of changes through slower nodes than relational databases. It is not recommended, therefore, to use this type of database for sensitive applications where updating the data must be instantaneous as in a bank, while it is suitable for a social network where millions of users are assumed.

Let's see what are the main pros and cons of NoSQL:

Pros	Cons
Flexibility and scalability	Data integrity
Simple and fast	A standard is missing
Maintenance	Not very mature and not very supported

In the next chapter we will see what are the strengths of MySQL compared to other competitors and why it is so widespread.

Advantages of MySQL

MySQL is one of the open-source databases that resists despite the development and production of new modern and high-performance databases. It allows a rapid planning and realization of the database allowing a rapid development of Web applications and guaranteeing access to thousands of Web users.

It is a database that seems to be created just to launch your project in the shortest possible time, starting from the rapid installation that we will see in the next chapter.

MySQL is a minimal database with only the essential functions but let's see together what are its strengths:

• The SQL standard: MySQL offers a standard environment and represents the first step to start with a database (it's a bit like when you start programming, you start from Assembly language not from Haskell);

• Easy to install: it is an essential and fast database with a quick installation. Being written in C and C ++ it is compatible with all operating systems and all platforms and during the installation it is also possible to configure a server administration section;

• Speed: MySQL does not require very powerful hardware; in fact it is possible to install it even on devices like Raspberry or old PCs as it does not make heavy use of system resources. Given its speed it is often used for websites, usually through CMS like Joomla and Wordpress;

• Community: MySQL cares about users' needs (thanks to its open-source nature) and demonstrates this in every new major release. Anyone who is expert in C and C ++ can analyze the source code and contribute to the improvement of this product;

• Interfaces: you can write an application in any language and easily integrate the MySQL database thanks to dedicated libraries, they exist for C, Java, PHP, Ruby etc.

A typical installation is composed of a MySQL Server that manages the data and a Client that will connect to the server to execute the queries. In large applications the server and the client reside on two distinct terminals but in small and medium-sized applications they can both reside on the same terminal.

The development environment

Installing MySQL

The MySQL installation starts with the installation of the server with which it is possible to manage the privileges of the various users, the server itself and its functionalities.

For all operating systems it is possible to download the appropriate file from the following link:

https://dev.mysql.com/downloads/windows/installer/8.0.html to get the Community Edition.

Since it is an open-source project, it is possible to compile the source code based on your server, allowing an increase in performance but this is recommended only to those who have experience in this field since it is easy to incur errors, even more in Windows and macOS.

For all others and for those who want to concentrate on MySQL only, we recommend following our guide.

Once connected to the link above, we download the software by clicking on "Download".

Once the download is complete, launch the executable and, after accepting the license agreement, choose the type of Developer Default installation that will install MySQL server and some useful tools.

In the next screen two sections will be shown: in the left one the available components will be present while in the right one the components that will be installed.

If you intend to integrate MySQL into an application select in the Connectors branch the one suitable for your programming language.

In the next screen, dedicated to the initial configuration, we will have to select Standalone MySQL Server / Classic MySQL Replication proceed with Next and then select Development Machine if we want to install the database on a PC to develop, Server Machine if it is a dedicated server (web server) o Dedicated Machine if it is a dedicated database server.

We select the TCP / IP entry and make sure that the port is set to 3306.

We select Strong Password and then specify the root password of the database, keep it in mind because it's really important: it's the password of the user with the maximum privileges.

Now we have to decide how and when the server will be started. Check the first entry so that MySQL runs as a Windows service and, if you think it is necessary, check the second entry to start the database when the PC starts, otherwise you can start it from the Windows Task Manager. We leave the Standard System Account flag selected and proceed with the configuration.

We won't enable the X / MySQL as protocol in the Document Store.
In the following screen the configuration steps will be performed and, once successfully completed, we can select both items to launch MySQL Workbench and MySQL Shell.

MySQL Workbench? What is it?
MySQL Workbench is basically a graphical editor that allows you to connect to MySQL databases to run queries, start or stop the service we have configured, easily modify the tables or their structure. We will not use this tool for the purposes of our guide but I advise you to

explore it after becoming familiar with the database and you will realize its potential.

At this point the installation is finished and we can verify the installation by looking in the Windows MySQL 8.0 Command Line Client menu and once started will ask you for the root password.

If the installation was successful, the service is started and the password is correct, this window will appear:

Mac

Once connected to the link https://dev.mysql.com/downloads/mysql/,
let's download the software by clicking on "Download".

MySQL Community Server 8.0.15

Select Operating System:

| macOS | ▾ |

Looking for previous GA versions?

🔔 Packages for Mojave (10.14) are compatible with High Sierra (10.13)

| **macOS 10.14 (x86, 64-bit), DMG Archive** | 8.0.15 | 213.7M | **Download** |
| (mysql-8.0.15-macos10.14-x86_64.dmg) | | MD5: 4f6e618ec3964b0052831a5c3a40d26d | Signature |

After downloading the .dmg file, double-click to mount the image disk
and view its contents. The guided procedure will show the license
agreement to be accepted and then reach where we want to install as
shown in the following image:

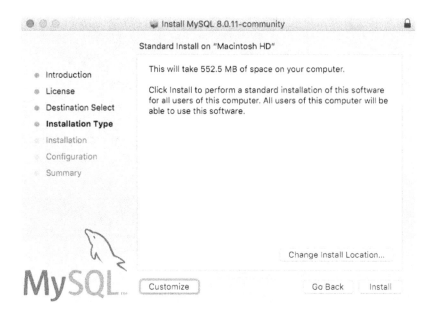

After choosing the path we must select the features to be included in the installation:

After installing MySQL Server you need to define the type of password to use (we recommend *Strong Password Encryption*):

Configure MySQL Server

- Introduction
- License
- Destination Select
- Installation Type
- Installation
- **Configuration**
- Summary

○ **Use Strong Password Encryption**

MySQL 8 supports a new, stronger authentication method based on SHA256. All new installations of MySQL Server should use this method.

Connectors and clients that don't support this method will be unable to connect to MySQL Server. Currently, connectors and community drivers that use libmysqlclient 8.0 support the new method.

○ **Use Legacy Password Encryption**

The legacy authentication method should only be used when compatibility with MySQL 5.x connectors or clients is required and a client upgrade is not feasible.

Next

Go Back   Continue

Then you need to define the password for the root user: the one who has the highest privileges:

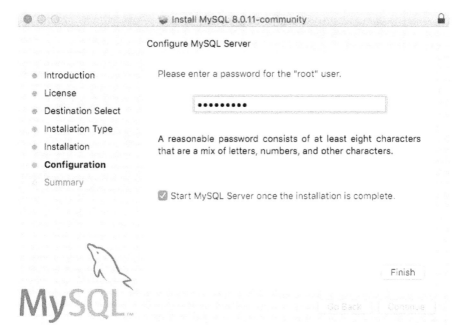

At this point, if the MySQL installation is successful, you can check the status of the server through the terminal with the command **mysql.server status**, if started you can enter the MySQL console through the command

mysql -u root -p

If everything has been installed correctly you will see this in your shell:

```
Enter password:
Welcome to the MySQL monitor.  Commands end with ; or \g.
Your MySQL connection id is 8
Server version: 8.0.11 MySQL Community Server - GPL

Copyright (c) 2000, 2018, Oracle and/or its affiliates. All rights reserved.

Oracle is a registered trademark of Oracle Corporation and/or its
affiliates. Other names may be trademarks of their respective
owners.

Type 'help;' or '\h' for help. Type '\c' to clear the current input statement.

mysql>
```

Linux

For Linux users the installation is really very simple, in fact you can do everything via the terminal.

Create a folder, move inside it and make a *wget* with the following commands:

cd /mysql/

wget   https://dev.mysql.com/get/mysql-apt-config_0.8.12-1_all.deb

sudo dpkg -i mysql-apt-config_0.8.12-1_all.deb

You will be asked what you want to install, make sure you install the MySQL server and, if you plan to create an application, you can also install the associated tools and connectors as in the image:

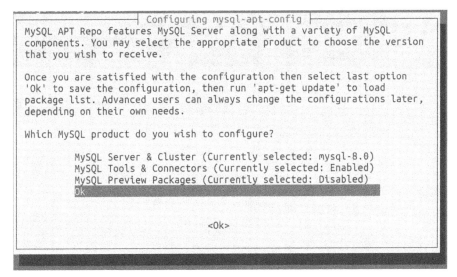

Now that the repository is installed, execute these commands from the terminal to launch the installation:

sudo apt update

sudo apt install mysql-server mysql-client

In this way the latest version of MySQL will be installed and you will be asked for the password for the root user or the one who has the highest privileges:

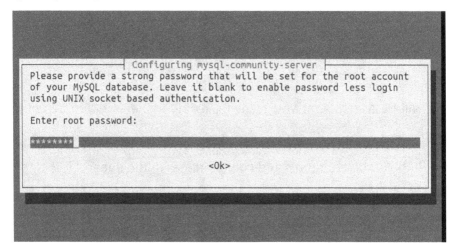

You will also be asked what type of authentication to use (we suggest

Strong Password Encryption):

```
-------------------------| Configuring mysql-community-server |-------------------------
  Select default authentication plugin

    Use Strong Password Encryption (RECOMMENDED)
    Use Legacy Authentication Method (Retain MySQL 5.x Compatibility)


                                   <Ok>

```

Once the installation is complete, you can log in as root with the

command:

sudo mysql -u root -p

Enter the root password set previously and, if there are no errors, this

will be shown:

```
root@ip-172-31-44-56:/home/ubuntu# mysql -u root -p
Enter password:
Welcome to the MySQL monitor.  Commands end with ; or \g.
Your MySQL connection id is 5
Server version: 5.7.22-0ubuntu0.16.04.1 (Ubuntu)

Copyright (c) 2000, 2018, Oracle and/or its affiliates. All rights reserved.

Oracle is a registered trademark of Oracle Corporation and/or its
affiliates. Other names may be trademarks of their respective
owners.

Type 'help;' or '\h' for help. Type '\c' to clear the current input statement.

mysql>
```

Let's start

We analyzed extensively about how rapid development is with this database but, as with all things, before starting we carry out a design in order to make our structure simpler and leaner. How should a database be designed? To start with, it is fundamental to have the database context in mind, let's use an example to make the idea better.

We will create a database to store the grades of university students for each course, we could create a simple table of this type:

```
+---------+---------+-----------------+------+
| Name    | Surname | CourseName      | Grade |
+---------+---------+-----------------+------+
| John    | Doe     | English         |   28 |
| Mark    | White   | Programming     |   30 |
| George  | Green   | Programming     |   29 |
+---------+---------+-----------------+------+
```

This type of table is not optimized: in fact a first limit is found in the case of homonymy: if there are two Mark White, to whom we are referring?

For this purpose we can introduce a unique ID (key) to overcome this problem so the table would look like this:

```
+----+---------+---------+-----------------+------+
```

ID	Name	Surname	CourseName	Grade
1	John	Doe	English	28
2	Mark	White	Programming	30
3	George	Green	Programming	29

You may think that, at this point, the table is perfect, but no. In fact, Mark White took an exam twice, the first obtaining a low grade (15) and the second with 30. With the current structure, unless a complex key with all the fields involved, it is not possible to insert this information.

We could insert new columns that indicate the year and the semester but it is necessary however to implement a better solution.

Two distinct tables could be created, one with student details (ID, Name and Surname) and one with details of the exams (student ID, CourseName, Grade).

By implementing a good design from the beginning of the design, many refactoring and subsequent modifications can be avoided.

Who designs a database should be able to distinguish between entities and attributes. Entities are objects of interest to the database, for example, a user's mobile number is hardly an entity of the DB.

If an object has multiple instances that need to contain data then the object will be an entity just as it is important to evaluate whether the object will often be null. In the case of null objects it would be better to model it as an entity rather than as a frequently empty attribute.

Database

Show and Create

After the database design phase we start with the practical phase that we will face here and in the next chapters. It all starts with the creation of a database so after logging in to MySQL as root, we can see which databases are present and create new ones.

We can see which databases are defined by the following command:

```
mysql> SHOW DATABASES;
+--------------------+
| Database           |
+--------------------+
| yard_management    |
| information_schema |
| mysql              |
| performance_schema |
| sys                |
| world              |
+--------------------+
6 rows in set (0.00 sec)
```

And create a new database with the name my_application by:

```
mysql> CREATE DATABASE my_application;
      Query OK, 1 row affected (0.08 sec)
```

In this case we are sure that the database does not already exist but if we were not to be so MySQL meets us with the following command:

```
      mysql> CREATE DATABASE IF NOT EXISTS my_application;
      Query OK, 1 row affected (0.10 sec)
```

Use

Now that we have created the database, we need to tell MySQL that we want to work with this database:

```
      mysql> USE my_application;
      Database changed
```

Drop

Unfortunately, at the time of typing I misread the database name so I want to delete it completely and recreate it. Warning! This operation will delete all the tables that the database contains, its references, indexes, columns, disk references to that database used by MySQL.

```
mysql> DROP DATABASE my_applicaton;
Query OK, 0 rows affected (0.18 sec)
```

The number of rows returned in the answer indicates the number of tables removed, in my case it is zero because I had not yet defined tables.

Also for this command it is possible to verify that the database exists before proceeding with the cancellation. If the database does not exist you will receive a MySQL error of this type:

```
mysql> DROP DATABASE my_application;
ERROR 1008 (HY000): Can't drop database
'my_application'; database doesn't exist

mysql> DROP DATABASE IF EXISTS my_application;
Query OK, 0 rows affected, 1 warning (0.05 sec)
```

At this point, after deleting the database with the wrong name, I recreate it with the correct name and try to query the system to see if there are any students.

```
mysql> SELECT * FROM students;
ERROR 1146 (42S02): Table 'my_application.students'
doesn't exist
```

I got an error because there is not yet an entity (table) with this name
in the database so we will continue with the creation of the tables.

Tables

This section explores the structure of the tables, in particular, we will show how:

• Choose table names and create them

• Understand and choose the column types suitable for the attributes

• Understand and choose keys and indices

• Use the AUTO_INCREMENT function

Create

We are ready to create the *student* table*:*

```
mysql> CREATE TABLE IF NOT EXISTS student (
    -> student_id SMALLINT() NOT NULL DEFAULT ,
    -> student_name CHAR(128) DEFAULT NULL,
    -> PRIMARY KEY (student_id)
    -> );
Query OK, 0 rows affected (0.41 sec)
```

Although MySQL reports 0 modified lines we can verify that the table has been created:

```
mysql> SHOW TABLES;
+---------------------------+
| Tables_in_my_application  |
+---------------------------+
| student                   |
+---------------------------+
```

```
1 row in set (0.01 sec)
```

Well, we've created the *student* table with two attributes: student_id and student_name.

But let's see in detail: the syntax for attributes is: *name type [NOT NULL | NULL] [DEFAULT value]*.

The name refers to the name of the column, a maximum of 64 characters long (like the name of the database) and punctuation and blank spaces are not allowed except the character _.

The type refers to the data that will be stored, that is, **CHAR** for the strings, **SMALLINT** for the numbers, **TIMESTAMP** for date and time.

The possible data types are many and now we will give a brief description for the most used ones:

• INT [(length)] [UNSIGNED] [ZEROFILL] is one of the most used types to store integer values from -2,147,483,648 to 2,147,483,647, if there is the UNSIGNED clause the range varies from 0 to 4,294,967,295.

The length indicates the size of the number and is used especially with ZEROFILL to insert 0s to the left of the value (eg 0022 for an INT (4) ZEROFILL);

• DECIMAL [(length [, decimals])] [UNSIGNED] [ZEROFILL] is used for non-integer numeric values such as distance or quantity. By declaring

DECIMAL (4,2) values from -99.99 to 99.99 can be used. The UNSIGNED and ZEROFILL clauses perform the same job as previously seen;

• DATES used for historicizing dates and can accept different formats:

or YYYY-MM-DD, YY-MM-DD eg 2019-04-30

or YYYY / MM / DD, YYYY: MM: DD, YY / MM / DD

or YYYY-M-D, YYYY-MM-D, YYYY-M-DD

or YYYYMMDD or YYMMDD

• TIME used for time logging and can accept different formats:

or DD HH: MM: SS, HH: MM: SS, DD HH: MM, HH: MM, DD HH, or SS where DD indicates the days

or H: M: S

or HHMMSS, MMSS and SS

• TIMESTAMP that stores the date and time in the formats:

o YYYY-MM-DD HH: MM: SS or YY-MM-DD HH: MM: SS

or YYYYMMDDHHMMSS or YYMMDDHHMMSS

• CHAR [(length)] is one of the most used types and stores values of defined length. If the length is not defined it takes 1 as the default value while the maximum value is 255.

Specifying NOT NULL the line must necessarily have a value for this column otherwise the data entry procedure will fail. If this clause is omitted the column may have no values.

The DEFAULT clause is used to set a default value for the column when no other data is provided.

Finally we have defined a primary key that is a unique value that identifies every single row in the table. In this way an index is created whose purpose is to speed up the search using the primary key.

We can see the indexes created in a table:

```
mysql> SHOW INDEX FROM student;
+---------+------------+----------+-----------------+---
---------+----------+...
| Table | Non_unique | Key_name | Seq_in_index |
Column_name | Collation |...
+---------+------------+----------+-----------------+-
---------+----------+...
| student |   | PRIMARY |   | student_id | A |...
+---------+------------+----------+-----------------+-
---------+----------+...
... +------------+----------+----------+------+------
------+---------+
... | Cardinality | Sub_part | Packed | Null |
Index_type | Comment |
... +------------+----------+----------+------+------
------+---------+
... |   | NULL | | | | BTREE | |
... +------------+----------+----------+------+------
------+---------+
  row in set (    sec)
```

39

Insert

Data entry into tables is usually done when adding data via an application or when bulk data is loaded by batch.

It is essential to know the structure of the table before insertion and this is possible through the command:

```
mysql> SHOW COLUMNS FROM student;
+---------------+---------------+------+-----+--------
-+-------+
| Field         | Type          | Null | Key | Default
| Extra |
+---------------+---------------+------+-----+--------
-+-------+
| student_id    | smallint(5)   | NO   | PRI | 0
|       |
| student_noma  | char(125)     | YES  |     | NULL
|       |
+---------------+---------------+------+-----+--------
-+-------+
2 rows in set (0.09 sec)
```

40

Let's assume we want to include two students in this table, Mary, John and Frank:

```
mysql> INSERT INTO student VALUES (1, 'Mary');
Query OK, 1 row affected (0.13 sec)


mysql> INSERT INTO student VALUES (2, 'John');
Query OK, 1 row affected (0.10 sec)


mysql> INSERT INTO student VALUES (2, 'Frank');
ERROR 1062 (23000): Duplicate entry '2' for key
'PRIMARY'
```

We got an error because we tried to add a new line with ID equal to 2 in the table and this is not allowed in relational databases.

We correct the statement and re-run it:

```
mysql> INSERT INTO student VALUES (3, 'Frank');
Query OK, 1 row affected (0.10 sec)
```

You might be tempted to insert a higher ID dynamically but you will get an error because you can't read and write to the same table at the same time:

```
mysql> INSERT INTO student VALUES ((SELECT
1+MAX(student_id) FROM student), 'Frank');
ERROR 1093 (HY000): You can't specify target table
'student' for update in FROM clause
```

AUTO_INCREMENT

To overcome this problem MySQL has the AUTO_INCREMENT function that allows the creation of a unique identifier for each line even without knowing the last identifier entered.

We delete the previous table and recreate it with AUTO_INCREMENT:

```
mysql> DROP TABLE IF EXISTS student;
Query OK, 0 rows affected (0.25 sec)

mysql> CREATE TABLE student (
    -> student_id SMALLINT() NOT NULL
AUTO_INCREMENT,
    -> student_name CHAR(125) DEFAULT NULL,
    -> PRIMARY KEY (student_id)
    -> );
Query OK, 0 rows affected (0.37 sec)
```

Now we can insert lines inside the table passing NULL as the first parameter:

```
mysql> INSERT INTO student VALUES (NULL, "Mary");
Query OK,  row affected (    sec)

mysql> INSERT INTO student VALUES ("John");
ERROR      (   S01): Column count doesnt match value
count at row

mysql> INSERT INTO student VALUES (NULL, "John");
Query OK,  row affected (    sec)

mysql> INSERT INTO student VALUES (NULL, "Frank");
Query OK,  row affected (    sec)

mysql> SELECT * FROM student;
+--------------+----------------+
| student_id   | student_name   |
+--------------+----------------+
|            | Mary           |
|            | John           |
|            | Frank          |
+--------------+----------------+
  rows in set (    sec)
```

As we have seen, a new unique ID is declared with each new line inserted. The keyword AUTO_INCREMENT tells MySQL that if no value is provided for the column student_id, a value greater than the maximum currently stored in that column in that table must be assigned.

The AUTO_INCREMENT function has the following requirements:

• The column on which it is used must be indexed;

• On the column with AUTO_INCREMENT there cannot be a DEFAULT;

• Only one AUTO_INCREMENT column can be used per table.

Select

For each entry MySQL will inform us about how many rows have been entered correctly, however, we can verify how many rows are present in a table using the following command:

```
mysql> SELECT * FROM student;
+--------------+----------------+
| student_id   | student_name   |
+--------------+----------------+
|            1 | Mary           |
|            2 | John           |
|            3 | Frank          |
+--------------+----------------+
3 rows in set (0.00 sec)
```

The output consists of three lines, each with a different student_id and a student_name, we could also select which columns to show as output:

```
mysql> SELECT student_name FROM student;
+----------------+
| student_name   |
+----------------+
| Mary           |
| John           |
| Frank          |
+----------------+
3 rows in set (0.00 sec)
```

We now introduce a new clause that is very simple to use but really useful for applying a filter.

Suppose we want to retrieve all student information with ID equal to 3:

```
mysql> SELECT * FROM student WHERE student_id = 3;
+------------+--------------+
| student_id | student_name |
+------------+--------------+
|          3 | Frank        |
+------------+--------------+
1 row in set (0.00 sec)
```

If we look for an ID that does not exist, MySQL obviously returns an empty set:

```
mysql> SELECT * FROM student WHERE student_id = 4;
Empty set (0.00 sec)
```

After making the MySQL query returns all the elements that respect the filter, in this case only one.

We can also select all the students who are called John:

```
mysql> SELECT * FROM student WHERE student_name = 'john';
+------------+--------------+
| student_id | student_name |
+------------+--------------+
|          2 | John         |
+------------+--------------+
1 row in set (0.00 sec)
```

As you can see, although I searched for *john* in the filter, MySQL returned the line where the name is *John*, which indicates that the database is case-insensitive when it comes to search.

Let's go on with the common searches, we look for all those who have an ID less than 3:

```
mysql> SELECT * FROM student WHERE student_id < 3;
+------------+--------------+
| student_id | student_name |
+------------+--------------+
|          1 | Mary         |
|          2 | John         |
+------------+--------------+
2 rows in set (0.01 sec)
```

47

We are looking for all the students who have a different ID than 1:

```
mysql> SELECT * FROM student WHERE student_id <> 1;
+------------+--------------+
| student_id | student_name |
+------------+--------------+
|          2 | John         |
|          3 | Frank        |
+------------+--------------+
2 rows in set (0.00 sec)
```

We insert other elements in the table to have a more substantial table and perform a search with AND and OR conditions. In particular in the first select we look for the student with ID equal to 4 and named Rocco, in the second we look for the student named Mark or the student with ID equal to 2.

```
mysql> INSERT INTO student VALUES (4, 'Rocco');
Query OK, 1 row affected (0.12 sec)

mysql> INSERT INTO student VALUES (5, 'Albert');
Query OK, 1 row affected (0.13 sec)

mysql> INSERT INTO student VALUES (6, 'Brad');
Query OK, 1 row affected (0.09 sec)

mysql> INSERT INTO student VALUES (7, 'Nicholas');
Query OK, 1 row affected (0.08 sec)
```

```
mysql> SELECT * FROM student WHERE student_id = 4
AND student_name = 'Rocco';

+------------+---------------+
| student_id | student_name  |
+------------+---------------+
|          4 | Rocco         |
+------------+---------------+
1 row in set (0.00 sec)

mysql> SELECT * FROM student WHERE student_name =
'Brad' OR student_id = 2;

+------------+---------------+
| student_id | student_name  |
+------------+---------------+
|          2 | John          |
|          8 | Brad          |
+------------+---------------+
2 rows in set (0.00 sec)
```

Update

Suppose we want to update a value within the previously defined table. ID 6 does not refer to the student Brad but to the student named Jordan.

```
mysql> UPDATE student SET student_name = 'Jordan'
WHERE student_name = 'Brad';
Query OK, 1 row affected (0.09 sec)
Rows matched: 1  Changed: 1  Warnings: 0
```

MySQL tells us that it has found only one line named Brad and has made the requested change on one line.

Delete

In the event that we wanted to start a new academic year or a new degree course we could eliminate all the lines or just some of them. If we do not add any filters, all the rows contained in the table will be deleted:

```
mysql> DELETE FROM student;
Query OK, 7 rows affected (     sec)
```

We can delete some lines for example, we will only delete students with ID greater than 5.

```
mysql> DELETE FROM student WHERE student_id >  ;
Query OK,   rows affected (      sec)

mysql> SELECT * FROM student;
+---------------+----------------+
| student_id    | student_name   |
+---------------+----------------+
|               | Mary           |
|               | John           |
|               | Frank          |
|               | Rocco          |
|               | Brad           |
+---------------+----------------+
   rows in set (      sec)
```

Drop

Deleting a table is very simple in MySQL and is fundamental in the reorganization of the database structure:

```
mysql> DROP TABLE IF EXISTS student;
Query OK, 5 rows affected (0.26 sec)
```

Sort functions

Limit

The LIMIT clause is a non-standard tool for checking which rows are returned as output and is mostly used when we wish to limit the amount of data to be transmitted over a network.

It can be used, for example, to show only 2 students via a Web application:

```
mysql> SELECT * FROM student;
+--------------+----------------+
| student_id   | student_name   |
+--------------+----------------+
|            1 | Mary           |
|            2 | John           |
|            3 | Frank          |
|            4 | Luis           |
|            5 | Mark           |
+--------------+----------------+
5 rows in set (0.00 sec)

mysql> SELECT student_name FROM student LIMIT 2;
+----------------+
| student_name   |
+----------------+
| Mary           |
| John           |
+----------------+
2 rows in set (0.00 sec)
```

This clause is particularly useful when the table contains many lines, saving buffering costs. It is also possible to show the first Y lines starting from the X position with the following command:

```
mysql> SELECT student_name FROM student LIMIT 2, ;
+----------------+
| student_name   |
+----------------+
| John           |
| Frank          |
| Luis           |
+----------------+
 rows in set ( .   sec)
```

Like

Sometimes it is necessary to find the matches of strings starting with a prefix, suffix or simply containing a string.

For example we want to search for all student names that have the suffix "K", this is possible thanks to the LIKE clause:

```
mysql> SELECT * FROM student WHERE student_name LIKE
'%K';
+--------------+----------------+
| student_id   | student_name   |
+--------------+----------------+
|            3 | Frank          |
|            6 | Mark           |
+--------------+----------------+
2 rows in set (0.00 sec)
```

The LIKE clause is used only with strings and serves to satisfy the specified schema, for example, we used '%K' to indicate zero or more characters followed by the K string.

Often the wildcard% is used to indicate all possible strings.

The same thing is possible to search for strings with prefixes:

```
mysql> SELECT * FROM student WHERE student_name LIKE
'Jo%';
+--------------+----------------+
| student_id   | student_name   |
+--------------+----------------+
|            2 | John           |
|            6 | Jordan         |
+--------------+----------------+
2 rows in set (0.00 sec)
```

Another wildcard that you can use is the underscore (_) character that maps exactly the length of the word we are looking for example:

```
mysql> SELECT * FROM student WHERE student_name LIKE
'J____';
+--------------+----------------+
| student_id   | student_name   |
+--------------+----------------+
|            2 | John           |
|           12 | Jony           |
+--------------+----------------+
2 rows in set (0.00 sec)
```

Now that we know the main conditions for filtering the results of a generic query we begin to combine them with logical operators in order to create more complex queries.

We are looking for all students with names that do not start with M with length 5 and that do not start with A.

```
mysql> SELECT * FROM student WHERE student_name
    -> NOT LIKE 'J____'
    -> AND student_name NOT LIKE 'A%';
+--------------+----------------+
| student_id   | student_name   |
+--------------+----------------+
|           3  | Mark           |
|           5  | Jordan         |
|           6  | Rocco          |
+--------------+----------------+
3 rows in set (0.00 sec)
```

We are looking for all the students in whose name the string is present *rk:*

```
mysql> SELECT * FROM student WHERE student_name LIKE
    '%RK%';
+--------------+----------------+
| student_id   | student_name   |
+--------------+----------------+
|           1  | Mark           |
|           3  | Barkus         |
+--------------+----------------+
4 rows in set (0.00 sec)
```

Order by

So far we have seen how to filter the result but not how it is represented. MySQL has the ORDER BY clause which is used to sort the results only during the display phase so the table will not be reorganized in any way.

The syntax is really simple and "talking":

```
mysql> SELECT * FROM student ORDER BY student_name;
+--------------+----------------+
| student_id   | student_name   |
+--------------+----------------+
|              | Mary           |
|              | John           |
|              | Frank          |
+--------------+----------------+
  rows in set (      sec)
```

The clause requires the column on which to execute the sort that will be used as a key and in our example we have chosen student_name.

The default sorting, that is without any parameter after the column name, is case insensitive and in ascending order since we are dealing with strings therefore from A to Z.

We introduce a new column to the student table that we will also use for the next functions, the column that we introduce represents the

59

average grade of the student and can be NULL in case the student has not taken any exam.

Let's add some values for the newly created column:

```
mysql> ALTER TABLE student ADD COLUMN average_rank
DECIMAL( , ) DEFAULT NULL;
Query OK,  rows affected ( .   sec)
Records:    Duplicates:    Warnings:

mysql> SELECT * FROM student;
+------------+----------------+------------+
| student_id | student_name   | average_rank|
+------------+----------------+------------+
|          | Mary          |        NULL |
|          | Frank         |        NULL |
|          | John          |        NULL |
+------------+----------------+------------+
 rows in set ( .   sec)

mysql> UPDATE STUDENT SET average_rank =   .   where
student_id =  ;
Query OK,  row affected ( .   sec)
Rows matched:    Changed:    Warnings:

mysql> UPDATE STUDENT SET average_rank =   .   where
student_id =  ;
Query OK,  row affected ( .   sec)
Rows matched:    Changed:    Warnings:
```

......

After adding some values the situation is as follows:

```
mysql> SELECT * FROM student;
+----------------+----------------+-------------+
| student_id     | student_name   | average_rank|
+----------------+----------------+-------------+
|              1 | Mary           |       23.44 |
|              2 | Frank          |       28.83 |
|              3 | John           |        NULL |
+----------------+----------------+-------------+
3 rows in set (0.00 sec)
```

Let's go back to the ORDER BY clause and look for the average votes ordering them from the highest to the lowest:

```
mysql> SELECT average_rank FROM student ORDER BY
average_rank DESC;
+-------------+
|average_rank|
+-------------+
|       28.83 |
|       23.44 |
|        NULL |
+-------------+
3 rows in set (0.00 sec)
```

Through the DESC keyword after the column to be sorted we have ordered the values in descending order.

If in in the average_rank column there are two equal values, to avoid this collision we can sort the values based on multiple columns. In our example we will order the columns by average grade and student's name.

```
mysql> SELECT average_rank, student_name
    -> FROM student
    -> ORDER BY average_rank, student_name DESC;
+------------+----------------+
|average_rank| student_name   |
+------------+----------------+
|       NULL | John           |
|      23.44 | Mary           |
|      28.83 | Frank          |
|      28.83 | Mark           |
+------------+----------------+
4 rows in set (0.00 sec)
```

So far we have seen some clauses and queries on a single table but in the next chapter we will create relationships between tables useful for "crossing" the data and creating a well-structured database.

Relations between tables

Let's now move from single-table queries to multiple tables. To better understand our examples we assume that each student has a tutor at his disposal and a tutor can follow more students.

We create the tutor table with the information of the tutor and the IDs of the students that follows:

```
mysql> CREATE TABLE IF NOT EXISTS tutor (
    -> tutor_id SMALLINT( ) NOT NULL AUTO_INCREMENT,
    -> tutor_name CHAR(   ) NOT NULL,
    -> stud_assigned SMALLINT( ) ,
    -> PRIMARY KEY (tutor_id),
    -> FOREIGN KEY (stud_assigned) REFERENCES
student(student_id)
    -> );
Query OK,   rows affected (    sec)

mysql> INSERT INTO tutor VALUES (NULL, 'Tutor 1',
 );
Query OK,   row affected (    sec)

mysql> INSERT INTO tutor VALUES (NULL, 'Tutor 1',
 );
Query OK,   row affected (    sec)

mysql> INSERT INTO tutor VALUES (NULL, 'Tutor 1',
 );
Query OK,   row affected (    sec)
```

```
mysql> INSERT INTO tutor VALUES (NULL, 'Tutor 2',
4);
Query OK, 1 row affected (0.07 sec)

mysql> INSERT INTO tutor VALUES (NULL, 'Tutor 3',
5);
Query OK, 1 row affected (0.05 sec)

mysql> INSERT INTO tutor VALUES (NULL, 'Tutor 3',
6);
Query OK, 1 row affected (0.09 sec)

mysql> INSERT INTO tutor VALUES (NULL, 'Tutor 3',
7);
ERROR 1452 (23000): Cannot add or update a child
row: a foreign key
constraint fails (`my_application`.`tutor`,
CONSTRAINT `tutor_ibfk_1`
FOREIGN KEY (`stud_assigned`) REFERENCES `student`
(`student_id`))

mysql> INSERT INTO tutor VALUES (NULL, 'Tutor 4',
NULL);
Query OK, 1 row affected (0.09 sec)

mysql> SELECT * FROM tutor;
+----------+------------+---------------+
| tutor_id | tutor_name | stud_assigned |
```

```
+-----------+-------------+-----------------+
|         1 | Tutor 1     |               1 |
|         2 | Tutor 1     |               2 |
|         3 | Tutor 1     |               3 |
|         4 | Tutor 2     |               4 |
|         5 | Tutor 3     |               5 |
|         6 | Tutor 3     |               6 |
|         7 | Tutor 4     |            NULL |
+-----------+-------------+-----------------+
7 rows in set (0.00 sec)
```

The creation of the table is similar to the one used for the student table but we have used an extra constraint: we have indicated to MySQL that the stud_assigned column exists which refers to the student table and in particular to the column named student_id.

We populated the table by entering the name of the tutors and the students assigned to each tutor, but when we assigned Tutor 3 to the student with ID 7, we received an error.

The error is fairly descriptive or MySQL reports that a student with an ID of 7 has not been defined so it cannot be assigned to a tutor.

Using the LEFT JOIN clause if a row of table 1 corresponds to a row of table 2 this is selected and coupled to the corresponding row, if instead there is not a corresponding row in table 2 this is coupled with a NULL row.

The Venn diagram helps us better understand how the LEFT JOIN works. We must consider the intersection of the two circles plus the whole area that is part of T1:

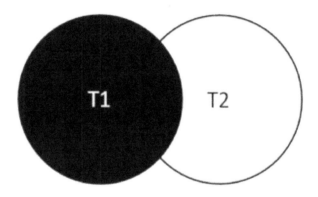

Now let's translate what we said in the SQL syntax:

```
mysql> SELECT t.tutor_name , s.student_name
    -> FROM tutor t
    -> LEFT JOIN student s
    -> ON t.stud_assigned = s.student_id;
+--------------+----------------+
| tutor_name   | student_name   |
+--------------+----------------+
| Tutor        | Mary           |
| Tutor        | John           |
| Tutor        | Frank          |
| Tutor        | Rocco          |
| Tutor        | Valery         |
| Tutor        | John Mary      |
| Tutor        | NULL           |
+--------------+----------------+
 rows in set (    sec)
```

In this case we note that we have defined an alias for both the tutor and student tables, respectively t and s. Creating aliases allows us to write queries faster.

The result, instead, shows what we have explained previously, every line that finds a correspondence with the table of the students is coupled, the line that refers to Tutor 4 does not find coupling and therefore is combined with NULL.

69

The INNER JOIN clause has substantially the same structure as the LEFT JOIN but returns a different result. With the INNER JOIN, reference is made only to the rows in table 1 that find a correspondence in table 2. In the following Venn diagram we must consider the intersection of the two circles, that is the part colored in black:

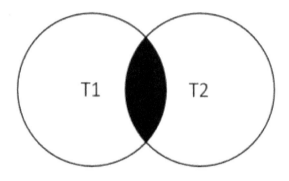

Also in this case we translate in SQL what we have seen graphically:

```
mysql> SELECT t.tutor_name , s.student_name
    -> FROM tutor t
    -> INNER JOIN student s
    -> ON t.stud_assigned = s.student_id;
+--------------+----------------+
| tutor_name   | student_name   |
+--------------+----------------+
| Tutor 1      | Mary           |
| Tutor 1      | John           |
| Tutor 1      | Frank          |
| Tutor 2      | Rocco          |
| Tutor 3      | Valery         |
| Tutor 3      | John Mary      |
+--------------+----------------+
6 rows in set (0.00 sec)
```

In the result we do not see Tutor 4 because it does not have a student assigned but for all the others there is a correspondence.

Right join

The RIGHT JOIN clause is practically identical to the LEFT JOIN but on the contrary all the rows in table 2 will be selected. Those that have a correspondence in table 1 will be shown associated to the value of table 1, those without correspondence will be associated with NULL.

To show the effectiveness of this clause we have included the student Phil who does not have an associated tutor and does not have an average grade.

We will note that all students will be returned and for each of them there will be a reference tutor except for Phil who is the last added and for him in the tutor_name column we will find NULL.

```
mysql> INSERT INTO student VALUES (NULL, 'Phil',
NULL);
Query OK, 1 row affected (0.16 sec)

mysql> SELECT t.tutor_name , s.student_name
    -> FROM tutor t
    -> RIGHT JOIN student s
    -> ON t.stud_assigned = s.student_id;
+-------------+----------------+
| tutor_name  | student_name   |
+-------------+----------------+
| Tutor 1     | Mary           |
| Tutor 1     | John           |
| Tutor 1     | Frank          |
```

```
| Tutor 2      | Rocco          |
| Tutor 3      | Valery         |
| Tutor 3      | John Mary      |
| NULL         | Phil           |
+--------------+----------------+
7 rows in set (0.00 sec)
```

Aggregation functions

Aggregation functions are particularly useful for discovering the characteristics of a group of rows. We can know how many rows there are in a table, eliminate duplicate rows, find maximum and minimum and average. In our example we will analyze these functions and in particular we will find the lowest average grade of all students, the highest average grade and much more.

MIN

The MIN function is very simple to use and returns the minimum value in a column. Only the values defined and therefore different from NULL are considered.

In this case we will return the lowest average rating but it also works with strings in fact it will return the first name in alphabetical order:

```
mysql> SELECT MIN(average_rank) FROM student;
+-------------------+
| MIN(average_rank) |
+-------------------+
|             22.00 |
+-------------------+
1 row in set (0.03 sec)

mysql> SELECT MIN(student_name ) FROM student;
+--------------------+
| MIN(student_name ) |
```

```
+--------------------+
| Mary               |
+--------------------+
1 row in set (0.00 sec)
```

MAX

The MAX function is exactly the opposite of the MIN function as we will see from the following examples:

```
mysql> SELECT MAX(average_rank) FROM student;
+------------------+
| MAX(average_rank) |
+------------------+
|            29.50 |
+------------------+
1 row in set (0.00 sec)


mysql> SELECT MAX(student_name ) FROM student;
+--------------------+
| MAX(student_name ) |
+--------------------+
| Valery             |
+--------------------+
1 row in set (0.00 sec)
```

AVG

Returns the average of the values in the specified column for all rows in a column. In our example we will return the average of the students' average marks, obviously the AVG function does not consider the NULL values and does not work on the columns containing strings in fact it will return 0.

```
mysql> SELECT AVG(average_rank) FROM student;
+------------------+
| AVG(average_rank) |
+------------------+
|          26.520000 |
+------------------+
1 row in set (0.00 sec)

mysql> SELECT AVG(student_name ) FROM student;
+--------------------+
| AVG(student_name ) |
+--------------------+
|                  0 |
+--------------------+
1 row in set, 4 warnings (0.00 sec)
```

SUM

The SUM function returns the sum of the values of the rows in a column or in a group. Let's think about how this function can help in a table with thousands of records and so we will have an idea of the work that MySQL does for us.

We will calculate the sum of the average marks of all the students and then calculate the sum of the average marks of students with ID less than 4.

```
mysql> SELECT SUM(average_rank) FROM student;
+-------------------+
| SUM(average_rank) |
+-------------------+
|            132.60 |
+-------------------+
1 row in set (0.00 sec)

mysql> SELECT SUM(average_rank) FROM student WHERE
student_id < 4;
+-------------------+
| SUM(average_rank) |
+-------------------+
|             74.27 |
+-------------------+
1 row in set (0.00 sec)
```

COUNT

The COUNT function returns the number of rows in a column or group with specific conditions. The COUNT function, unlike the others, takes into account both NULL and non-NULL values. Let's count how many rows there are in our two tables: students and tutors.

```
mysql> SELECT COUNT(*) FROM student;
+----------+
| COUNT(*) |
+----------+
|        7 |
+----------+
 row in set ( .   sec)

mysql> SELECT COUNT(*) FROM tutor;
+----------+
| COUNT(*) |
+----------+
|        7 |
+----------+
 row in set ( .   sec)
```

Specifying the column on which you want to perform the COUNT will only count non-NULL values.

```
mysql> SELECT * FROM student;
+------------+--------------+--------------+
| student_id | student_name | average_rank |
+------------+--------------+--------------+
|          1 | Mary         |        23.44 |
|          2 | John         |        28.83 |
|          3 | Frank        |        22.00 |
|          4 | Rocco        |        29.50 |
|          5 | Valery       |        28.23 |
|          6 | John Mary    |         NULL |
|          7 | Phil         |         NULL |
+------------+--------------+--------------+
7 rows in set (0.00 sec)

mysql> SELECT COUNT(average_rank) FROM student;
+---------------------+
| COUNT(average_rank) |
+---------------------+
|                   5 |
+---------------------+
1 row in set (0.00 sec)
```

We count how many students named Mary exist in our table:

```
mysql> SELECT COUNT(average_rank)
    -> FROM student
    -> WHERE student_name = 'Mary';
```

```
+------------------+
| COUNT(average_rank) |
+------------------+
|                1 |
+------------------+
1 row in set (0.00 sec)
```

DISTINCT

When querying tables, it is possible that there are duplicate rows as we noted earlier for some values of the average student grade.

In this case we can delete these values by adding the DISTINCT clause to the SELECT in order to filter these cases.

```
mysql> SELECT average_rank FROM student;
+--------------+
| average_rank |
+--------------+
|        23.44 |
|        28.83 |
|        22.00 |
|        29.50 |
|        28.83 |
|         NULL |
|         NULL |
+--------------+
7 rows in set (0.00 sec)

mysql> SELECT DISTINCT average_rank FROM student;
+--------------+
| average_rank |
+--------------+
|        23.44 |
|        28.83 |
|        22.00 |
```

```
|        29.50 |
|         NULL |
+--------------+
5 rows in set (0.00 sec)
```

It is evident that the duplicate values inside the column were two, 28.83 and NULL. With the DISTINCT clause we have eliminated these values only during the visualization of the result, the data inside the table have not been altered in any way.

GROUP BY

This clause is usually used to create subgroups of lines as a summary of line values or expressions. GROUP BY returns a single row for each group and in practice reduces the number of rows in the result set. In particular we can consider it useful when we have a shopping list and we want the total amount of food, the total amount of detergents, the total number of household items, etc. but they are all contained in a single list. This clause must appear after the FROM and WHERE clauses as in the example:

```
mysql> SELECT average_rank, COUNT(*)
    -> FROM student
    -> WHERE student_id <= 6
    -> GROUP BY average_rank;
+--------------+----------+
| average_rank | COUNT(*) |
+--------------+----------+
|        23.44 |        1 |
|        28.83 |        2 |
|        22.00 |        1 |
|        29.50 |        1 |
|         NULL |        1 |
+--------------+----------+
5 rows in set (0.00 sec)
```

In this example we have searched all the students with ID less than or equal to 6 and we have grouped them by average grade and it emerged that two of them have an identical average grade or 28.83.

HAVING

Another important clause for data aggregation is HAVING, which is usually used together with a SELECT to specify the filter of a group of rows.

This clause must always be placed after the GROUP BY otherwise it behaves as a simple WHERE condition. The difference between the two is that HAVING applies the filter to a group of lines (this is why it makes sense after a GROUP BY) while WHERE applies the filter to each single line.

The university decides to promote the first 6 registered students with an average higher or equal to 28.
Since you manage the database the request is addressed to you that you will have to carry out the requested extraction.

We can take the previous example by adding a condition, that is, we are looking for all students with ID less than 7 (ie less than or equal to 6), grouping them by average grade and having an average grade greater than 28.

```
mysql> SELECT average_rank, COUNT(*)
    -> FROM student
    -> WHERE student_id <= 6
    -> GROUP BY average_rank
    -> HAVING average_rank >= 28;
+--------------+----------+
| average_rank | COUNT(*) |
+--------------+----------+
|        28.83 |        2 |
|        29.50 |        1 |
+--------------+----------+
2 rows in set (0.00 sec)
```

The university decides to promote the first 6 registered students with an average higher or equal to 28.

Since you manage the database the request is addressed to you that you will have to carry out the requested extraction.

We can take the previous example by adding a condition, that is, we are looking for all students with ID less than 7 (ie less than or equal to

6), grouping them by average grade and having an average grade greater than 28.

IS NULL

The university decides to consult students who have not yet passed any exam to understand where they encounter the greatest difficulties, therefore they ask you for an extraction with relative names of students and tutors.

To execute this query, we will have to select the name of the tutor and of the student, make a join between the two tables involved and look for users who have an average NULL value.

Let's perform this query in our database:

```
mysql> SELECT t.tutor_name , s.student_name
    -> FROM tutor t
    -> RIGHT JOIN student s
    -> ON t.stud_assigned = s.student_id
    -> WHERE s.average_rank IS NULL;
+--------------+----------------+
| tutor_name   | student_name   |
+--------------+----------------+
| Tutor 3      | John Mary      |
| NULL         | Phil           |
+--------------+----------------+
2 rows in set (0.00 sec)
```

As we can see Phil does not have a tutor assigned so the tutor's name will be NULL.

MySQL Workbench

What is it?

After learning the syntax and applying it through the terminal, we make it even easier by showing MySQL Workbench.

This tool allows you to administer, create and modify a database, all its tables, constraints and keys defined through a graphic editor.

We can greet the display of the command line and we can see the tables defined in a completely new look and, perhaps, more pleasing to the human eye.

During the installation of the Workbench a connection was automatically created so open the program called "MySQL Workbench 8.0 CE" and this is what you will see:

If there are no defined connections, press the + button to add new ones.

Click on the instance shown and you will be asked for the root user password.

At this point you will find a side panel where your databases are defined including my_application which we defined at the beginning.

By clicking on the databases you can see the structure, their tables, indexes, keys, etc..

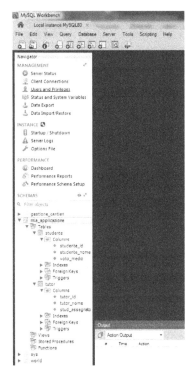

Selecting a table, right-click and selecting the first item: Select Rows - Limit 1000 will automatically query the database and return the first 1000 rows.

Amazing, right? Moreover, you can modify the values directly inside the cells without going through the SQL syntax, the editor will take care of generating and executing the right query for you.

Suppose we want to change the value of the average Valery rating, just double click in the cell, update the value and press the Apply button on the right as in the image.

In case we had performed an operation by mistake, do not panic, we can go back at any time thanks to the Revert button.

The section above the results display can be understood as a real console so we can write our queries there and press the lightning icon to run it.

On the left side, between the various commands of MANAGEMENT, we find *Server status* that allows us to monitor the status of our MySQL server or how many connections are active, how much CPU is used and many other useful information to monitor the health and load of the database.

In the section dedicated to *Client Connections* it is possible to see the details of each connection established and, if necessary, order its destruction. In addition to the administration section of the users and their privileges, a section dedicated to the database and system variables.

Regarding the import and export of the database there are two distinct entries, both of which allow you to import / export a database from / to a folder or from / to a file and you can choose to import / export only the database structure and tables, only the data or both.

As for export, there is a section dedicated to advanced options which is very useful for speeding up and customizing exported queries.

In the INSTANCE section we find a simple start and stop of the instance, the logs that are used to verify the operations performed by the database and any errors and the instance configuration file.

MySQL also gives us an idea of the PERFORMANCE of our database in the appropriate section, here are shown in real time the data on incoming and outgoing traffic expressed in Bytes / second and the total number of connections. It also informs us about the status and efficiency of the cache as well as the number of SELECT, INSERT, CREATE, UPDATE, ALTER, DELETE and DROP per second. These parameters will be very useful when our application will be used by many users simultaneously and will allow us to understand which queries to optimize and which data to cache.

Conclusions

At this point, in our MySQL book, we hope that you have become familiar with the system and hope you have not encountered any major difficulties. The SQL syntax is not very hard to understand and is quite "talking". Continue to practice and with experience you will be able to face new challenges, many more complex queries than those proposed by us.

With this book the main objective was to provide a smattering of the main and most important functions of MySQL, we have deliberately omitted. We have neglected the management of users and their privileges, such as backing up and restoring the database, the performance cost of a query but they are all topics intended for advanced users who already know the database and its components well.

For further information you can follow the official documentation at the following link: https://dev.mysql.com/doc/refman/8.0/en/.

All registered trademarks and logos mentioned in this book, including Amazon, belong to their respective owners.

The author of this book does not claim or declare any rights to these trademarks, which are mentioned only for educational purposes.

.

www.ingramcontent.com/pod-product-compliance
Lightning Source LLC
LaVergne TN
LVHW051715050326
832903LV00032B/4225